TIM DeLeon &
JONATHAN DeLeon

VISUAL PRICING
FOR REAL ESTATE

THE SIMPLE 5 STEP PROCESS FOR REAL ESTATE PRICING THAT TAKES
THE CONFUSION OUT OF PUTTING TOGETHER AND PRESENTING CMAs.

Dedication

This book is dedicated to the most amazing and successful woman I have ever had the pleasure of knowing. Joanne DeLeon, my wonderful mother and the wife of Tim DeLeon, is without a doubt the reason that this book exists. Not only is she the founder of Focus 1st LLC, the person who spoke on a stage to sell CDs, and the Visual Pricing System's biggest success story, but she shows me every day what a real estate professional aspires to be. Her love for and dedication to clients, and their happiness, are undeniable. Having the blessed chance to witness someone like her pouring her mind and soul into real estate is a true gift.

Jonathan DeLeon
Focus 1st LLC

Table of Contents

1

Introduction and Backstory

Introduction and Backstory

It was a normal, weekday, late night at the office. The cleaner's vacuum could be heard buzzing down the hallway of the nearly empty ghost town. Only one real estate agent remained at this hour. That agent was Tim DeLeon, staring at a computer screen, trying to figure out a puzzle. He was pricing a house for a pre-listing appointment, and while this should be a simple and fast process, Tim was not your typical real estate professional.

He had recently joined the ranks of real estate professionals after a twenty-five-year career in electrical engineering. This background had made a profound impact on his thinking. While his training in home sales had taught him a massive bank of sales techniques and buzzwords, his mind was wired differently. For him, the question of how much a house was worth was no simple task. It was a formula with a lot of variables. It was a formula that must have a solution. The "old-school" tactic of picking three comparables and adjusting up and down seemed archaic and *incomplete*.

Earlier that day, while talking to the customers he was preparing this pre-listing CMA for, Tim had been asked a simple question: "When is the best time to sell my house?"

Most salespeople would have replied, "With me, any time is good," or, "Now," followed by a curt smile and a wink. Tim couldn't do that. Like I said, he was wired differently. He replied simply, "I'll find out." There had to be an actual answer, and he was the man to find it.

Well he did find that answer, and he also found the answers to a number of other key customer questions. Those answers became part of a process he formulated, which allowed him to do something that most others couldn't. He was able to transcend traditional pricing and create pricing strategies. These strategies were so responsive and accurate that a powerhouse real estate agent in the company took notice. This agent happened to be his wife, Joanne DeLeon.

Soon Joanne was using this pricing-strategy process to explode her already immensely successful business. The combination of this amazing new type of home-value analysis and Joanne's natural sales ability and emotional connection with her clients led to an atmospheric rise. Before long, everyone at the company wanted to understand how this process worked. Focus 1st

LLC was created to help spread knowledge and tools. But now, for the first time, in these pages, we are spreading the knowledge of how to create a pricing strategy in a format separated from a software purchase. We are doing this because we know that it will help real estate professionals.

I know the information in these pages will help you for two reasons. First, we have had the pleasure of helping real estate professionals all across the US and Canada over the past nine years. We have given them tools and education, and watched many of them grow their businesses by leaps and bounds. They have learned how to accurately price and predict competition while building a strategy that is reactive to the market. This combination leads to more closings and a better business.

The second reason I know this text will help you is also the reason I'm 100 percent confident in that claim. A few years after Joanne DeLeon used the tools to catapult her business, I did the same. I was not an already successful agent at the company. I was a ground-zero *rookie*.

I started with nothing. I barely had a contact list. Most of my friends were still in college or one year out.

Buying and selling houses was in their five-to-ten-year plan. I needed to get something going in the next five to ten weeks. So I used this pricing process to win almost every listing appointment I received. Competition from more experienced real estate agents didn't mean anything compared to my pricing strategies. I was able to be part of **twenty-six transactions that year**. How many of you would like to **add twenty-six closings to your business list this year?** I used pricing strategy to do that with no base. Imagine what you can do.

The next chapters will explain in detail this process we call *Visual Pricing for Real Estate*. You will first be given an overview of how the process works and then be given full education on each individual step. Read it. Commit it to your mind. This is a powerful tool that will be invaluable to your business. When you're done with this book and you close it, I ask you to do two things. First, <u>*use it!*</u> I want you to be another success story of *Visual Pricing for Real Estate*.

Second, I ask a favor. Please take a minute or two and post a review on Amazon.com. Books live and die by their reviews, and I sincerely want this book to spread across the real estate community.

Thank you very much for trusting us with your time. *It will be worth it.*

Sincerely,
Jonathan and Tim DeLeon

2

What Is Visual Pricing for Real Estate?

What Is Visual Pricing for Real Estate?

Visual Pricing for Real Estate, or *Visual Pricing* for short, is a process of accurately pricing and positioning a home for sale and then putting it all together into a powerful presentation. I want to emphasize that this is a process. This is not a simple "find the answer and you're done" method of pricing. It is a step-by-step pathway to establishing a pricing strategy. This strategy does more than find the market value of a house. It allows you to position the listing for max competitive impact, take into account neighborhood timing and even anticipate future competition. By taking these factors into account, along with value, you can not only really find an accurate price but also be able to predict the customer's selling experience—everything from how long it should take to sell their home to how many of their neighbors will move during the same time period.

Visual Pricing is also a way of thinking. As you go through the steps of this process, you are being led on a mental journey. You focus on the property you are pricing, zoom out to the big picture, and then—bit by bit—zoom back in. Eventually you will also look into a crystal ball and zoom past the current time and into the future. This metaphorical zooming in and seer saying is a powerful way of solving problems. It is borrowed from engineering school in many ways. The best way to find the solution to a problem, like pricing a house, is to first define what you're trying to find (the price of the home). Second, you define what you know and what you don't know (the house characteristics/location and the price/timing). Third, you relate them to each other (find patterns). Fourth, you add in possible error. This last step is where your analysis of the competition and pricing strategy really come into effect, essentially turning competition and new entrants into our possible-error scenario.

This may sound complicated and extremely time consuming, but once you have finished reading this book, you will be amazed at how simple it is. I am purely typing this detailed description of why the steps are organized in the way they are so that you know that there is a rhyme to the reason. The steps are put together in the way they are for a purpose.

Visual Pricing is also a way of presenting. The Visual Pricing steps lay out nearly perfectly with something many filmmakers refer to as the "Tarantino Way." By first focusing on the property we are selling, we start with a glimpse of the end. Then we lead the customers on a journey that starts with a wide camera view of the whole picture. The story progresses as we zoom and focus in on the smaller picture. Then we reach where we started, the house. The story isn't over though. We take the seller even farther down the road, into the future. By taking the seller on this mental journey, we are able to teach, entertain and connect on a deep level that solves what is often the most difficult factor in pricing strategy. What is that step? I'll get to that in a moment.

Visual Pricing for Real Estate is a six-step process.

Step 1: Know the Subject Property

The subject property refers to the home you are currently analyzing for sale. You must know the key details about the house in order to price it accurately, but more importantly, you need to understand what is *unique* about this property. You must know if the counters are upgraded, if the house sits on a busy street or if the neighborhood allows RV parking. You must be able to really nail down the details that make this house different from every other three-bed, two-bath in its neighborhood. We will be using that info, and <u>it is essential.</u>

Step 2: Know the Neighborhood

The neighborhood or area (for those of you who live in communities that don't use neighborhoods) is the most important feature of a property 70 percent of the time. "Location, location, location," became a common phrase for a reason. This step goes deeper, however: You must know how the area/neighborhood acts. What are its habits? Do houses sell only one month out of the year? Do houses sell here if they don't go under contract immediately? Know the patterns, and you'll know the neighborhood.

Step 3: Compare to Recent "Solds"

You may be more familiar with this step. Every real estate agent knows how to look at the last six months for comparable homes and adjust for positives and negatives. We elevate this technique to a higher level. No longer is it good enough to guesstimate the adjustments. You will find a pattern here first and then adjust from that baseline.

Step 4: Position with "For Sales" and "Soon-to-be For Sales"

This is where strategy really starts to show its beautiful face. Your goal when pricing a home is to find the ultimate sweet spot. You want the house to sell fast and for the most value. By putting yourself at a competitive advantage, you create a scenario where this is much more likely. This positioning is also proactive because we are going to look at the competition that is coming down the road.

Step 5: Connect Everything Together

In this step, we are taking all the previous steps and tying them together so that their relationship, the give and take, combine to create the complete pricing strategy. Only by looking at all the patterns can we find a combining point that is our final pricing strategy. Larry Kendall, founder of Ninja Selling, likes to make the comparison between using the Visual Pricing Process and an MRI. Actually, sometimes he refers to it as a Real Estate MRI. You look at different slices, but only by putting it all together do you see the complete picture.

Step 6: SECRET

I'm keeping this step a secret for now. This is the step that has become an invaluable tool for many real estate professionals. I am choosing not to tell you what the secret step is at this moment because I want you to read and understand the other steps first. This final step is the cherry on top of your pricing-strategy sundae. It is what wraps it all together, the ribbon on your present.

Do not skip ahead and cheat yourself of the full impact of this step. A cherry or ribbon by itself makes less sense and impact than when it is combined with the right pieces. Wait for it and you will better understand why this step is *so important.*

3

Why Should You Use the Visual Pricing Process?

Why Should You Use the Visual Pricing Process?

Visual Pricing has been proven, by real estate agents across the US and Canada, to be the most effective way to accurately price homes. This is because it achieves success in incorporating all the factors of pricing strategy, while other methods simply look at the factors of pricing. You may have heard that there are five factors in pricing.

These are the factors:
1. Location
2. Price
3. Size
4. Special Features & Amenities
5. Condition

These five factors help you determine the value of a house and therefore a price. What is required today is something different though. The market is too dynamic. *You must have a strategy.* Pricing strategy takes these five factors and adds three more in order to become all encompassing. The first factor added is **Timing**. Timing the market and understanding the pattern of your neighborhood is extremely important when it comes to accurately pricing a home for sale. The second factor added to the process is **Positioning.** The third factor added—and final in the process—is **Understanding**.

Understanding has been a more recently developed requirement. Today people are very different than they were just ten years ago. Much of this has been created by the growth of the internet and the "information age." When people don't understand something or have a question, they know that they can just Google it and find the answer. They are used to learning. This is where you must step in. Today, teaching your pricing is just as important as pricing accurately. This is where Secret Step 6 comes in… down the road.

These are now the eight factors in pricing strategy:
1. Location
2. Price
3. Size
4. Special Features & Amenities
5. Condition
6. Timing
7. Positioning
8. Understanding

Visual Pricing walks you through covering all eight factors of pricing strategy in its six steps. This process allows you to absolutely zero in and nail the price of your listing. What will this do for your business? Explode it.

You will have more transactions if you really use this process. Your listings will sell for more, sell faster and sell with less pain. These better transactions lead to better relations with customers and more referrals. Add this to the additional transactions you will accomplish by beating out other real estate agents for listings and you will be asking yourself how you ever sold real estate without Visual Pricing. I ask myself every day how so many agents do.

Well the time has come.

In the next chapter, you will find the first step of Visual Pricing, but here's one last thing before getting started.

As you read this book, you will find graphs that help show the patterns and information I speak about. These graphs were created using our software program, The Visual Pricing System. *Visual Pricing for Real Estate*, and its steps, dictated the creation of our software, so I'm going to use it to best show the steps. The steps, however, don't require using any specific software or following a computer program. The graphs are simply there for your understanding. If at any point you want to learn more about the software, it is available at www.focus1st.com. Please visit the website and check out everything we have if it's something that interests you.

I want this book to focus on teaching versus selling, but how could I not tell you about it at least once? I don't think I could have sold real estate without this tool, and I believe you should have the opportunity to know it exists. That being said, let's look at the first step in the Visual Pricing process.

4

Step 1: Know The Subject Property

Step 1: Know the Subject Property

Knowing the subject property may seem like a very simple and "elementary school level" step, but we all must start with the basics. Without the right foundation, a home will not stand up to the test of time. The same is true with our pricing process. If the first step itself is not solid, then the rest of our pricing will be flawed.

I can't even express to you the number of times real estate agents struggle to understand this step. Since we have been able to help real estate professionals all over with their CMAs, it's a problem that must be addressed immediately. *You must be able to fully understand and describe what the house you're pricing <u>IS</u>.*

So we are going to start here. We will lay out the process that makes up Step 1. Yes, that's right, we have processes inside of processes. I will expand most of the steps into additional steps. Don't worry, at the end of this book is a page that reviews all of the steps in a concise manner, labeled "The Visual Pricing Process." So let's get started.

Step 1.1

Let's start where most of your customers go to answer their questions: Google. (A quick note: We aren't sponsored by Google or anything like that. It's simply the most widely used search engine. If you have another search engine you prefer, then use that *if it has a mapping function*.) Search the address of your listing in Google Maps. You will see a regular map appear.

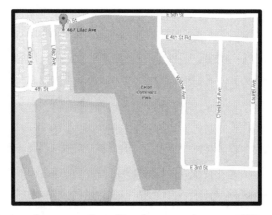

Click to change the display to the satellite image and then zoom in.

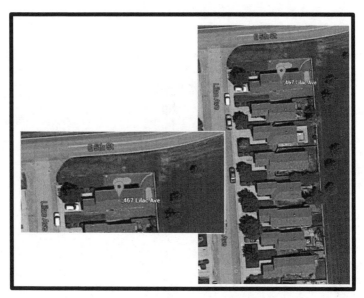

Now ask yourself, what can I see from this image? Ask yourself questions about the property itself. For example, is the house on a major thoroughfare? Is it a corner lot? Where on the lot does the house sit? How big is the yard? Is there on-street parking? Is the driveway larger than the two-car entrance or not?

Why are we asking these questions? Because they matter! They are important details of the home, just as important as if it has hardwood or carpet flooring.

Step 1.2

Now that we know what the outside of the house is like, it's time to go inside. I should clarify: It's time to go inside without actually *going* inside. We will accomplish this by looking at old MLS sheets and public records.

EXAMPLE MLS SHEET

EXAMPLE PUBLIC RECORDS

We are looking at these to get a clear picture of the characteristics that make up the home: square footage, bedrooms, etc. Some of you may be wondering, "Why both?" Well it's simple: *I don't trust MLS type-ups.* Although they are often more descriptive than public records, they are also often inaccurate because of either mistakes during data entry or exaggeration by the real estate agent. *MLS sheets are primarily a way to sell homes;* they always have some subjectivity in them. Public records are recorded law and are may be more accurate, although less complete. The combination of the two gives a fairly complete and fairly accurate picture.

Step 1.3

The third step is to complete a pre-listing interview. This is usually a phone call that consists of asking key questions about the subject property so that you can gain further understanding about the seller, their motivations and the current conditions of the property. Included in the pre-listing interview are questions such as, why are you selling? When do you need to move by? Have you done any updating to your property since you purchased it? How would you rate the condition of your home and property? For your convenience, we've included a pre-listing interview questionnaire that we've printed with permission from Ninja Selling (www.ninjaselling.com), one of the premier real estate training organizations in the country, in the back of this book.

Step 1.4

Now if you are doing this pricing after having visited the home in person, then you are done with the final step in the Knowing the Subject Property process.

If you have yet to visit the home and are doing a pre-listing pricing, then it's fine, but just know that you will be coming back to revisit this step.

When you visit the home, be sure to take a notebook or tablet computer with you. You will be taking little notes as you walk through. Write down anything and everything that you feel is an outlier from what you read in the MLS and public records or that you know is significant.

What has the current homeowner added that is uncommon or would increase the marketability of the home? Also note what things are strikingly negative and detrimental to the price. What is it about the property that makes it stand out in a good or bad way?

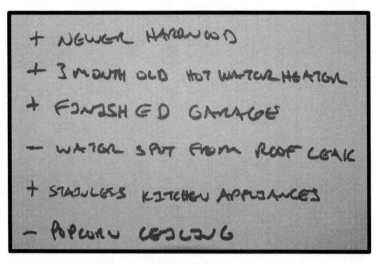

EXAMPLE OF HANDWRITTEN NOTES FROM
A BRIEF HOME WALKTHROUGH

Also, when you walk through the property, ask what is included in the sale. Are all the appliances staying? How about the hot tub?

One of the other key values you will want to provide to the seller is to help them better understand any changes they can make to the property that will make it more saleable, or more marketable. Many sellers don't realize how buyers will see their home. Things they have become completely accustomed to may be detractors in value. These changes often include some investment by the seller prior to putting their home on the market. Examples include making repairs to the roof, painting the exterior, replacing carpet, getting carpets steam cleaned, etc.

Assuming you have visited the home and have your list of positive and negative price influencers, you will combine these into the property description. All of these together give you a complete picture of the home.

Step 1.5

Full pictures are great, and we'll use that later on in the process; however, we are going to pull a few simple details out for Step 2. Actually, we will pull out one main detail: the location.

What is the name of the neighborhood (or area if you don't use neighborhoods) that your home is in?

Seventy percent of the time, this one answer will put us on the right path to answering the questions we need to answer.

We can easily find this on the old MLS sheet. *Fingers crossed the real estate agent spelled the neighborhood name correctly.*

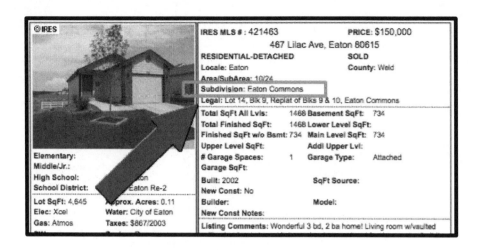

Do you have the answer to that question? Great, now we are going to take that answer and use it to perform **Step 2: Knowing the Neighborhood.**

5

Step 2: Know the Neighborhood

Step 2: Know the Neighborhood

Now that we know the name of the neighborhood, we are going to do some research on it. Again, in most cases, it's about *location, location, location*. The research we will do is meant to answer three key customer questions that give us the knowledge necessary to address the first factor of pricing (Location) and set up for the sixth factor of pricing (Timing) down the road.

We are going to learn more about the area by going into our MLS and searching for all information within that neighborhood.

Now, what if your area doesn't have neighborhoods or subdivisions? Many areas don't. In that case, we have found the best results by using the map function in your MLS to select the area. When using the map function, you will have several options for selecting the area. ***Do not use the radius function.*** We tend to see more errors using this method. The polygon or rectangle selection tool allows for much better data selection and customization.

When selecting the area using these tools, look for natural boundaries. Natural boundaries would include things like major streets, greenbelts, golf courses, mountains, lakes, etc. Once you've highlighted the area near the subject property using these boundaries, your search will include all the real estate activity in the relevant area.

Remember, 70 percent of the time, your search should be solely based on location. We do not want to prescreen here for square footage, bedrooms, etc. Simply search and pull out all the information by using either the neighborhood or map function as just discussed.

The other 30 percent of the time will occur when the property has something so unique about it that it would impact the sales experience greatly. Examples of this would include homes that sit on waterfront or golf courses, sit on abnormally large lots, etc. In these cases, you will need to include these search items along with location before getting all the information.

I just mentioned not prescreening for square-footage size. Why did I make a point of that? When we spend time with folks and help them with their CMAs, we find that most of the time when agents are "off" on their initial search, it is because they are limiting their search based on square footage of the home. Real estate agents usually constrain their searches based on homes that are plus or minus 10 percent of the size of the subject property. Most of this comes from the education that you need to compare the home to other properties that are comparable in size. This makes sense if all you are focused on is pricing the property. However, with Visual Pricing, while we will price the property, we are also going to determine our pricing strategy. So for this case, we need to understand what the current customer experience is in the location for all shapes and sizes.

So we go into our MLS and search for **ALL** the real estate activity in that neighborhood/area for the *last two years*. This means your search will include all Sold, Active (For Sale), Expired, Withdrawn, Under Contract, Terminated, Pending, or any other status items that your MLS may make use of. *NOTE: We are not interested in or including properties that are for rent or lease.*

It's not unusual for real estate agents we talk to on the phone to say, in an incredulous voice, "Two years of data? Are you saying we should price properties based on two-year-old information?" Of course not. However, we can't jump straight to pricing the home from the start.

To price accurately and with a strong pricing strategy, we need to see the trends over recent time frames. We can best do that with the past two years' complete status activity. This amount of information may seem daunting but is fully inclusive at this size. We will need this information to help build a clear picture. So how much information is this? We generally recommend that you look at fifty to one hundred properties when you include all status activity over the last two years. Now this is a guideline, and if we find thirty-five with one search, it's close enough. If we have 135, that's close enough as well. If we do need more data, we just expand the location/area that we are searching. If we need less data, we make the area smaller. Zoom out or zoom in. It's that simple. We find that when you hold on to this rough guideline, you have enough information to create a powerful pricing strategy that is clear and easy for the customer to understand and see.

Step 2.1

The first location pattern we are going to look for is what we call the "odds of selling." You must be able to tell your customer what the chances are that their house will sell. The key customer question usually sounds like, "Will my house sell?" This is one of the major doubts all sellers face. It may not be the most prominent, but it's always there in the back of their mind. Of course there are some cases where sellers assume that their home is going to sell no matter what. As real estate agents, we know better. There are plenty of homes that are withdrawn or expired (essentially properties that were priced above their perceived value), and you need to give them both the reality of their specific situation and the surety that this knowledge is based on real data, specific to their home.

So let's answer that question for them. We will do so by comparing the number of homes that have sold versus the total listings, including homes that were withdrawn, expired, are currently under contract, and are for sale but not under contract. We then convert that to a percentage.

On the next page is a simple, handwritten example for calculating this "odds of selling" number for one year of data. In most cases, we recommend looking at the last twelve months, the current calendar year's odds and the previous year's odds to help us identify patterns. The calculation method is the same for all three, so only the calculation for the last twelve months is shown on the next page.

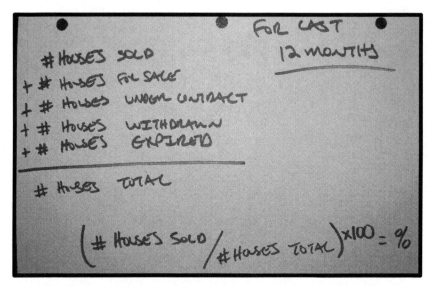

EXAMPLE OF HOW TO SET UP THE
CALCULATION

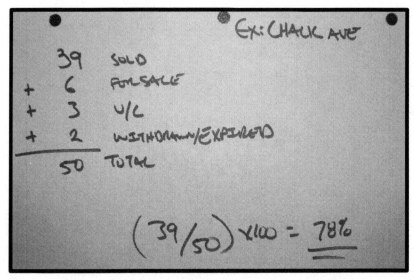

EXAMPLE CALCULATION

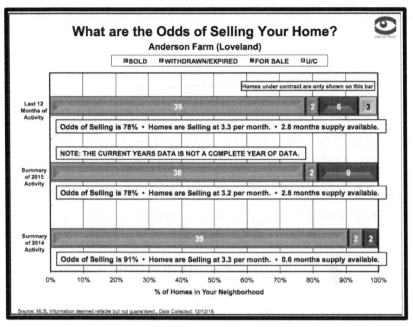

What are the Odds of Selling Your Home?

Anderson Farm (Loveland)

SOLD　WITHDRAWN/EXPIRED　FOR SALE　U/C

Homes under contract are only shown on this bar

Last 12 Months of Activity
39　2　6　3

Odds of Selling is 78% • Homes are Selling at 3.3 per month. • 2.8 months supply available.

NOTE: THE CURRENT YEARS DATA IS NOT A COMPLETE YEAR OF DATA.

Summary of 2015 Activity
38　2　9

Odds of Selling is 78% • Homes are Selling at 3.2 per month. • 2.8 months supply available.

Summary of 2014 Activity
39　2　2

Odds of Selling is 91% • Homes are Selling at 3.3 per month. • 0.6 months supply available.

0%　10%　20%　30%　40%　50%　60%　70%　80%　90%　100%

% of Homes in Your Neighborhood

Source: MLS. Information deemed reliable but not guaranteed. Data Collected: 12/12/15

EXAMPLE ODDS OF SELLING CHART

Note: In this graph, sold properties are represented by the large bar, blue when printed in color. Withdrawn and expired are represented by the bar reading 2, usually red. For sale are shown in the bar reading 6, usually green. And under contract are the light bar reading 3, printed as yellow when printed in color.

The chart above is one of those graphs I told you I would include. As you can see, the last twelve months' odds of selling is 78 percent on both the handwritten example and the chart example. The chart includes another way of calculating odds of selling, located in the white boxes below the colored bars. The result is the same, but we included it because many agents are big fans of this particular model.

This model is referred to as Absorption Rate Pricing. In this model, you calculate how quickly homes in the subject property's price range are selling. This calculation is also referred to as the absorption rate and is most commonly shown as homes sold per month.

$$\text{Absorption Rate} = \frac{\text{Number of Homes Sold}}{\text{Number of Months}}$$

For example, if there were fifteen homes sold in six months, the absorption rate would be as follows:

$$\frac{15 \text{ Homes}}{6 \text{ Months}} = 2.5 \text{ Homes/Month}$$

Once you figure out the absorption rate, you then look at the current supply in the same area and price range of homes for sale or under contract. You can then determine how long it will take to sell the current list of homes on the market. This is also referred to as the Months' Supply.

$$\text{Months' Supply} = \frac{\text{Number of Homes in Current Supply}}{\text{Absorption Rate}}$$

For example, if there were ten homes currently on the market or under contract and the absorption rate was 2.5 homes sold per month, the months' supply would be as follows:

$$\frac{10 \text{ Homes in Current Supply}}{2.5 \text{ Homes/Month}} = 4 \text{ Months' Supply}$$

Months' supply represents the length of time to sell the existing inventory if homes continue to sell at the same rate of sales and if there are no new properties put on the market. Of course, these are generally not good assumptions.

The National Association of Realtors® has stated that when the months' supply is six months, it is a balanced market. If the months' supply is less than six months, then it is moving to a seller's market. And if the months' supply is greater than six months, then it is moving to a buyer's market. Using this model, you can see how long it should take to exhaust the current supply of homes on the market and then use this to figure out your odds of selling in the period of time that is of interest to you.

Continuing the example, if you want to sell in a month, then we use this formula:

$$\text{Odds of Selling} = \frac{\text{Absorption Rate X 100 \%}}{(\text{Homes in Current Supply} + 1)}$$

In this case, the plus one (+1) is your home, and your odds of selling would be as follows:

$$\text{Odds of Selling} = \frac{2.5 \text{ X 100}}{(10 + 1)} = 23\%$$

The process above and the calculations work effectively when there is a uniform rate of sales across the year. This means that it works well if the same number of homes are sold consistently throughout the year. We've seen that this can be the case for areas that are located on either of the coasts, where markets are not seasonal. However, when you have markets that are seasonal, you need to consider this and make adjustments. You may need to make adjustments for market trends as well.

That actually leads us nicely into the second location pattern we are going to find: the buying pattern for this area. Every neighborhood has a pattern of sale. Some are in the summer, some in the winter, some in the fall and spring. We need to find this pattern to best answer the key customer question, "When is the best time to sell my house?"

Step 2.2

To find this pattern, we are going to take the dates of closing from all the sold properties and group them together by the month. Where do the sales cluster? Draw a box around the clustering times. There is our pattern.

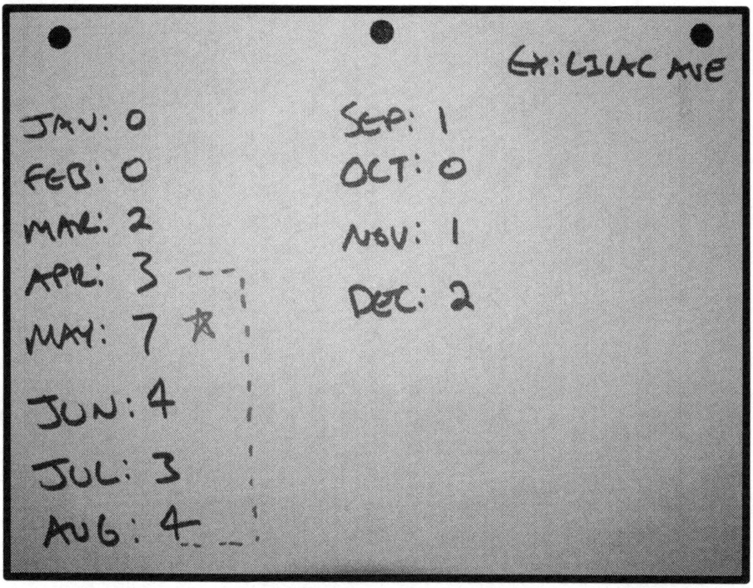

JAN: 0   SEP: 1
FEB: 0   OCT: 0
MAR: 2   NOV: 1
APR: 3   DEC: 2
MAY: 7
JUN: 4
JUL: 3
AUG: 4

EX: LILAC AVE

HAND DRAWN BUYING PATTERN

Be sure to keep your years separate here if you have two years' worth of information! Don't mix in two years of information, as patterns can change. If you want to go for extra credit, make a pattern for each of the years. Comparing these can show "hot selling times" shifting. If the neighborhood is shifting forward or backward, we want to know that!

Below is a graphical example of this relationship from the Visual Pricing System.

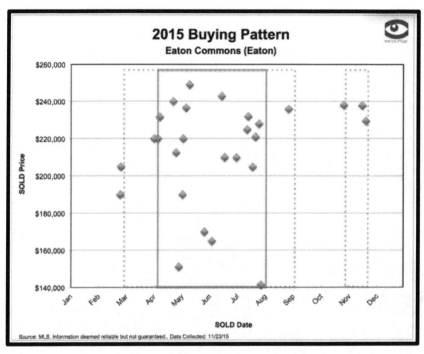

EXAMPLE BUYING PATTERN

This graph shows the clustering of a neighborhood in Northern Colorado. Obviously this is more accurate because it allows for information to be plotted mid-month. To do this in a non-automated style would take too long. One of the benefits of using software. However, notice that the buying window is still the same as our handwritten example.

Be aware that buying patterns can change over time for several reasons. It isn't unusual to see these patterns move slightly to the left or right due to weather patterns. However, when we present the graph to customers, we like to say, "While we don't know what this year's sales pattern will look like, we can look at last year's pattern and take action based on that information." Also remember, this pattern is based on actual sold dates. This means the date represents when they closed, so if we are looking at our property going on the market, we need to look forty-five to sixty days earlier to accurately account for under-contract time.

Step 2.3
The third location pattern we are going to find now is the average time to sell. This answers the key customer question, "How long will it take my house to sell?" Or more accurately, "How long should it take my

house to sell?" This pattern also illuminates something else that is important about the neighborhood. It shows us how price affects time to sell. If higher-priced homes take longer to sell, we should see that.

To find this pattern, take a look at all the listings that sold. The length of time between their closing and listing dates is the time it took for that house to sell. Yes, I know that closing date is not a perfect time variable, as often closings are scheduled differently for each transaction; however, it is accurate enough, on average, when you have enough information.

Let's see an example of this pattern identified by hand. It is a simple average taken of all the days to sale in the data for a subject property's location. We can now look at the houses that deviate farthest from this pattern and see if shorter periods correspond to lower price and longer periods to higher price.

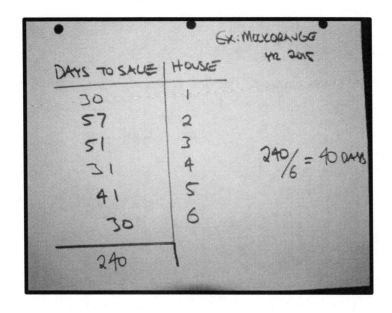

I used the software to show you a more detailed and complex example.

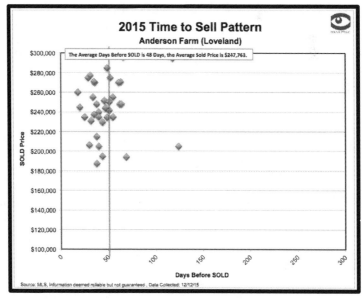

EXAMPLE TIME TO SELL GRAPH

As you can see, this property has a considerably larger set of data that we are looking at. However, the calculation for average time to sell is the same. In this visual representation of the pattern, it's easy to see how, if at all, price affects the average time to sell. We can also see how the houses tend to cluster around this time to sell. After this line, most homes don't sell. This can be taken into account later on down the line, when pricing strategy brings in timing.

The most important thing to notice here is how well we can predict the customer experience. If we price the home correctly and market it well, your listing should sell right around that forty-eight average-day mark or be under contract within the first three days!

After doing these calculations, we can now say with confidence that the area we are examining sells a certain percent of the time (78 percent from our chart example), most often in the month-to-month window (April-to-August window from our chart example), and it should take a certain number of days to sell (forty-eight days in our chart example.) We have answered three key questions and analyzed the area our listing is in.

We can say that we have a good grasp of the location. This factor of pricing is finished. That's one down. Now let's move on to Step 3: Compare to Recent "Solds" and address the next four factors in pricing before we move on to pricing strategy.

*A quick note: You may have noticed that the examples are different properties. I chose to do this to better show you variability. The important part is learning the process, not pricing one home specifically. **This process works in more than one case.**

6

Step 3: Compare to Recent "Solds"

Step 3: Compare to Recent "Solds"

Now it's time to look at what properties in our area have been selling for. This is the most traditional step of CMAs, consisting of finding and comparing recently sold houses to our subject property and adjusting up and down to better analyze the main pricing factors. The logic behind this is, if someone bought a home that was comparable to the subject property and paid a specific amount, then someone else would be willing to pay the same amount for the subject property.

To price properties, you must consider the five factors or characteristics of the property, mentioned earlier, as you compare them to other properties. First let's go a little more in detail on each of the five factors of pricing. You're familiar with these factors; however, a quick refresher will do us all good.

Pricing Factor 1

Location: Of course this is the most important characteristic of pricing properties. When you price properties, we recommend that you compare the subject property to other properties that are in the same location or neighborhood, as just discussed.

Pricing Factor 2

Price: When you price the subject property, you must consider what other homes have sold for. Of course, if other homes that are comparably sized to the subject property have sold for a specific amount, then they may dictate what the subject property will sell for.

Pricing Factor 3

Size: When you price the subject property, you must consider the size of other homes, especially as they compare to the subject property. What appraisers will do is limit the comparison homes to those that are within plus or minus 10 percent of the subject property. That is because they will then calculate the price per square foot to help identify the overall price of the subject property. This can create several inaccuracies. As we work with real estate agents across the nation, we often hear, "Price per square foot doesn't work in our area." Be aware when we price properties that we do not use price per square foot. We will use a visual comparison of the price and size that is much more effective than the old "price per square foot" comparison.

Pricing Factor 4

Special Feature and Amenities: This includes just about all the special things that differentiate homes. Generally we are looking for things that make the house different and may add significant value. If everyone in the neighborhood has a two-car garage and the subject has a three-car, this would be one of those features. Of course, if the subject property has a two-car, it would not be. Things to look for are hard-surface upgrades (both flooring and countertops); unique, location-specific things, such as backing to a greenbelt or backing to a major street; size or layout of the yard, which may be either a positive or negative; and other things that may be specific to your area. For older homes, we would include updating in this section as well.

Pricing Factor 5

Condition: The condition of the property would include things such as homes that are in foreclosure or short sales, homes that need TLC or haven't been well taken care of, homes that are used as rentals, or homes that have some other negative condition that would impact the property.

Now when we price properties, we love to put them on a scattergram. Scattergrams are great tools for seeing the correlation between price and size. In addition, if you restrict the properties that you put on the scattergram to homes in the area, it will take the location into consideration as well. Then if you will add a few comments on the scattergram to take into account the special features and condition of the property, you will find that you can summarize all five factors of how you price properties, on a scattergram, at one time in a very visual way. Let me say that again: With the scattergram, you can summarize all **five factors** of pricing on one chart. This is powerful for you and for your customers.

Visual Pricing differs from the traditional, old-school method in that we are not simply choosing three, or maybe a few more, and adjusting values up or down. We are going to use _all_ the recently sold homes in our area to populate our scattergram and then use that information to look for a trend line and adjustments.

Let's look at an example. Below is a list of *all the homes* that have sold in the Windshire subdivision in a *six-month period*.

Residential-Detached Listings

MLS #	Type	Price	Status	SqFt	Style	Beds	Area	Address
781604 IRES	RES	$289,999	S	2287	2 Story	3	10/23	1655 Merton Ct
773087 IRES	RES	$299,000	S	2484	2 Story	4	10/23	1663 Merton Ct
776441 IRES	RES	$311,000	S	2853	2 Story	4	10/23	1635 Kelmsley Ct
774677 IRES	RES	$325,500	S	3179	2 Story	4	10/23	560 Wycombe Ct
780220 IRES	RES	$348,500	S	3473	2 Story	3	10/23	600 Colney Ct
778503 IRES	RES	$418,000	S	4552	2 Story	4	10/23	612 Botley Dr
775030 IRES	RES	$430,000	S	4504	2 Story	5	10/23	635 Camberly Ct

Step 3.1

Now let's put them on a scattergram graph. We'll plot the prices on the y-axis (or the left) and the square feet on the x-axis (or the bottom). Plotting this on graph paper, we come up with a graph that looks like the image below.

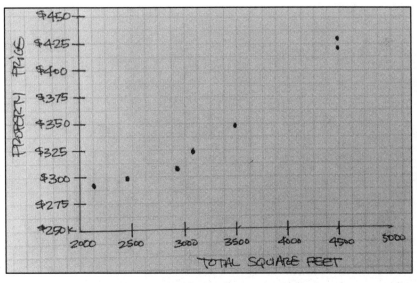

HAND MADE SCATTERGRAM

On this chart, we plotted the price the properties sold at on the y-axis and the size of the home (shown in Total Square Feet) on the x-axis.

Of course, the time to put together the scattergram chart isn't that difficult, and as you recall, we were taught how to do a scattergram in basic math. (Figuring out the scale on the axis takes the most work.) However, with computers, these charts can be easily and quickly created. Take a look at the chart we created using the Visual Pricing System.

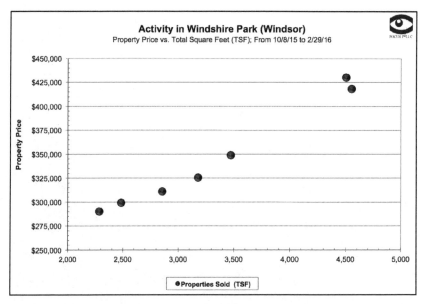

COMPUTER GENERATED SCATTERGRAM

Step 3.2

Since I'm using a computer, it's easy to add the trend line for this data. Doing this by hand requires some knowledge of basic algebra and a little patience. For now, we will stick to the computerized trend line in order to focus on its importance. To learn more about how to create this line by hand, refer to the end of this book, in the section titled *"Trend Line Calculating by Hand."*

Let's look at the chart with this trend line in place.

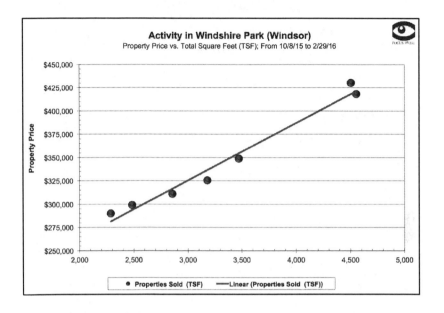

Activity in Windshire Park (Windsor)
Property Price vs. Total Square Feet (TSF); From 10/8/15 to 2/29/16

● Properties Sold (TSF)　▬Linear (Properties Sold (TSF))

Now with the trend line in place, we can easily see that for this area, there is a strong correlation between price and size. (All the data points are very close to the line.) For this reason, we also refer to this trend line as the "Fair Market Line." A correlating trend line shows the market relation between price and size.

It's not uncommon for folks to make the comparison between our Fair Market Line and purely pricing a home on a per square feet basis. A method, which is, talked about a lot of in the appraiser circles. Usually they'll say something like, "That doesn't work for us. You see pricing properties based on "price per square foot doesn't work for our area." Let me state clearly, *this is not the same as pricing properties based on price per square foot*. I'll expand and explain the differences a bit later.

Once we have a chart that looks like this, with the Fair Market Value line in place, it makes it very visual and pretty easy to price a property in any neighborhood.

Let me ask you, if you had a chart that looked like the previous scattergram for a property you wanted to price, could you easily see what that subject property would sell around? Of course you could. All you would have to know is the size of the subject property. Then find that value on the Square Foot axis below and draw a line straight up to where it intersects the trend line, just like we show below:

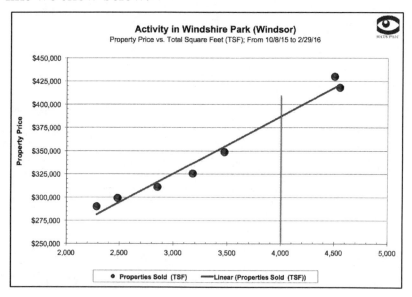

In the graph above, we are looking at what price a 4,000-square-foot home would sell for in this neighborhood. As you can see, it intersects the Fair Market Value line somewhere in the $385,000 to $390,000 price range. Additionally (and even more importantly), would you be able to show your customer this graph to help them see where they need to price their property to sell in this market?

Now let me address a couple of questions you may be having concerning the scattergram pricing charts and how to use them. The obvious first question is, "Do the graphs always come out looking like the one shown above, where all the data points are right on the line"? We have been helping agents all over the nation (and Canada) price properties in their areas, and while it is not uncommon to have a graph that looks very similar to this, there are also times when the dots on the graph do not fit perfectly on the line. (Notice that even on this graph, all the data points don't fit *perfectly* on the line.) Graphs tend to look like the previous one when all the properties plotted on the graph have comparable features and conditions.

When you create a scattergram and the data points are all over the chart, it generally means that many of the properties *are not comparable.* So what we are saying is that when you put together your scattergram, if the homes are comparable in features and conditions, they will always fall close to the line since the only difference is size. **Homes that are larger sell for more than homes that are smaller, everything else being equal.**

So let's restate this in a different way. When you create a scattergram graph and you find data points all over the chart, the reason for that is because there is something about the homes that is not comparable. And for you to do an effective job of pricing, you must discover what that is. So here are a couple of hints when using the scattergram. First look for the Fair Market Value line. Look for the data points that would create the trend line. When you find data points that are way off the Fair Market Value line, either way above or way below, there must be a reason. To do a great job pricing, you must find that reason.

In many cases, when you find a huge difference, the first thing we look for is location. While all the properties can be in the same neighborhood or area, when you have data points that are way off the Fair

Market Value line, if you look closely, you can find that several of the properties may have something significantly different based on their specific location. For example, there may be homes that are on waterfront while other homes are not. When we are helping others throughout North America, we will generally take a look at the properties using Google Maps (www.googlemaps.com) to see how the properties sit in the neighborhood and to identify location-specific values.

We can also find huge differences in properties based on views. This is a little different than location and may be more difficult to see. You may need to be more familiar with the area or may need to access a topographical map. When views are a big deal, it isn't uncommon for homes that are located across the street to differ greatly in price. We live in Colorado and know of a neighborhood where lots can differ in value as much as $250,000 because of the views of the mountains to the west.

In cases where the difference is still obvious but less major, look for condition or feature differences. This may take some close evaluation of the detailed MLS sheets to determine what the key differences are. Take a look at the Scattergram on the following page.

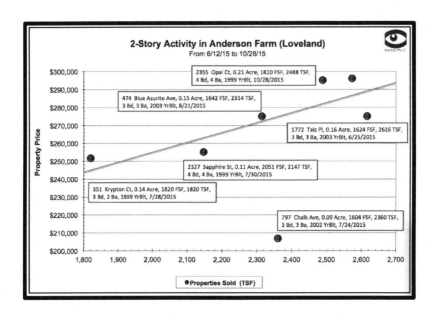

2-Story Activity in Anderson Farm (Loveland)
From 6/12/15 to 10/28/15

Property Price

- 2355 Opal Ct, 0.21 Acre, 1810 FSF, 2488 TSF, 4 Bd, 4 Ba, 1999 YrBlt, 10/28/2015
- 474 Blue Azurite Ave, 0.15 Acre, 1642 FSF, 2314 TSF, 3 Bd, 3 Ba, 2003 YrBlt, 8/21/2015
- 1772 Talc Pl, 0.16 Acre, 1624 FSF, 2616 TSF, 3 Bd, 3 Ba, 2003 YrBlt, 6/25/2015
- 2327 Sapphire St, 0.11 Acre, 2051 FSF, 2147 TSF, 4 Bd, 4 Ba, 1999 YrBlt, 7/30/2015
- 351 Krypton Ct, 0.14 Acre, 1820 FSF, 1820 TSF, 3 Bd, 2 Ba, 1999 YrBlt, 7/28/2015
- 797 Chalk Ave, 0.09 Acre, 1604 FSF, 2360 TSF, 3 Bd, 3 Ba, 2002 YrBlt, 7/24/2015

● Properties Sold (TSF)

Notice that in the graph, most of the data points are near the Fair Market Value line except the "797 Chalk" property (located near the $210,000 value). There must be a reason why that property sold so much lower than the Fair Market Value line. Additionally, you can see "2355 Opal Ct" sold for more than the Fair Market Value line and "1772 Talc" sold for less. The difference between these two properties will most likely be conditions and amenities. You may think that it's because of the difference of the four-bed to three-bed homes; however, if we look at "2327 Sapphire," which is also a four-bed house, we see that deviation from the trend line can't be solely due to bedrooms. Even with that extra bedroom, it is sold below the trend line. Obviously it is also less because of its square footage. Remember, *Size Matters!*

If your scattergram has a large number of outlier data points that seem to be all grouped together, then you may have found a daily double. Look for data points that would create another trend line parallel to the first but slightly up or down from it. Once you do that, you can then look for the differences between properties that are on both of the lines.

As you can imagine, after doing pricing analysis in many areas, we've found several key explanations for homes on the different trend lines that can be created.

Upgraded homes are a classic situation if you have an area of homes that are twenty years old or older. You might find that one set of homes may be in good shape and another set of homes may be in good shape and have also been updated. These properties will be on two different trend lines.

We've also found trend lines that are lower when you have homes that are distressed. These are homes that are under foreclosure or short sales, or just need TLC.

Step 3.3

As an example, look at the next scattergram. This graph was created by looking at all the properties sold in a six-month period in a specific neighborhood. When we first created the graph, all we saw were "a bunch of dots all over the graph."

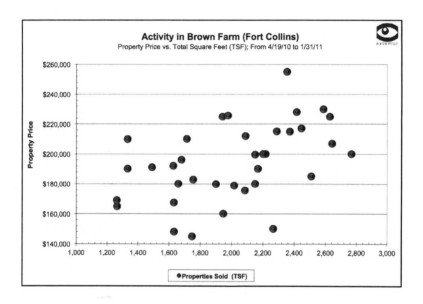

Scary, right? It's okay, we have seen graphs that look like this a fair number of times, as we help real estate professionals throughout the US and Canada. What do you do when you have a graph that looks like this? How can you price a property using that graph? Well what we usually do is take a closer look at the properties. In most cases, we focus on location. For this example, since they are all in the same neighborhood, the location will not provide the answer.

First, as we look at the graph, there is a lot of data there. As a guideline, we recommend that a pricing scattergram have five to seven of the *most* comparable properties. But that is a guideline, and we don't always stick to it. I'm sure you'll notice that many of the scattergram examples we show exceed that guideline. But how do we know what properties are most comparable?

Here is a snapshot of some of the actual data that was graphed. What do you notice?

Sold	2154	Ryeland Ln	1 Story/ranch	0.48	988	1976	1976	4	3	1976	$225,000
Sold	1943	Dorset Dr	Tri-level	0.15	1264	1264	1264	3	2	1974	$175,000
Sold	2407	Leghorn Dr	1 Story/ranch	0.16	1157	2245	2288	4	3	1979	$218,000
Sold	2118	Suffolk St	Bi-level	0.23	1756	1756	1756	4	2	1973	$179,000
Sold	1900	Corriedale Dr	Bi-level	0.14	816	1632	1632	4	2	1972	$154,900
Sold	2342	Hampshire Rd	1 1/2 Story	0.19	1670	2541	2641	3	3	1978	$209,900
Sold	2307	Suffolk St	Tri-level	0.16	1489	1489	1489	4	2	1974	$195,000
Sold	2036	White Rock Ct	2 Story	0.19	1399	1985	2084	4	3	1982	$183,900
Sold	2224	Clydesdale Dr	Four-level	0.25	1528	2088	2088	3	2	1983	$215,000
Sold	2700	Garden Dr	2 Story	0.21	1344	2016	2016	3	2	1983	$178,900
Sold	2200	Yorkshire St	1 Story/ranch	0.16	821	1630	1630	3	2	1983	$169,900
Sold	2530	Leghorn Dr	1 Story/ranch	0.18	1253	2353	2353	4	2	1979	$279,900
Sold	2219	Rambouillet Dr	Four-level	0.18	1654	1654	2200	3	3	1978	$215,000
Sold	2437	Farghee Ct	Bi-level	0.19	885	1700	1749	4	3	1978	$159,000
Sold	2454	Leghorn Dr	1 Story/ranch	0.21	1146	2000	2266	4	3	1979	$164,900

Taking a closer look at the data, you'll see that we have properties with different architectural/floor-plan styles. We have "1 Story/ranch," "Tri-Level," "Bi-level," "2 Story" and even "Four-level" properties on the same graph. When we price properties, we like to look at homes that are comparable. To compare homes that are comparable in this case, let's look at the homes that have the comparable architectural/floor-plan style. We'll just look at the properties that are "1 Story/ranch" properties for now.

We should note here that we don't always restrict comparisons to properties that are the same floor-plan style. Of course, if there are plenty of properties that have sold with the same floor plan as our subject property, then we'll stick to using only those comparables. However, when we are searching for properties to add to the graph, we don't see a big difference, from a customer viewpoint, between two-story and tri-level floor plans or even four-level plans. But we try not to include bi-level floor plans with others unless we must. We also like to keep the one-story/ranch plans by themselves as well. Again, this is a guideline, and as with all guidelines, we don't always adhere to it.

Once we remove all the other floor plans from the graph and use only the "1 Story/ranch" floor-plan data, we can create a graph that looks way more in the realm of normality, but it's not quite there yet. Initially, it looked like there was no correlation between the price and size at all. While there is less data (and therefore seemingly more manageable), there still doesn't seem to be a great pattern that will help price the subject property. Take a look at the graph now:

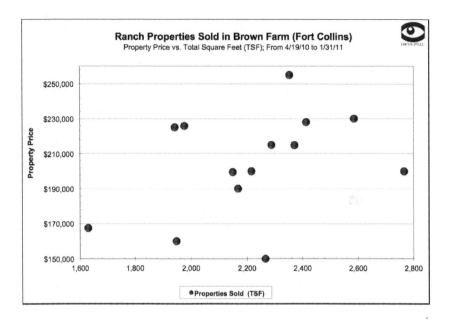

When you create these graphs and see data points all over, yet in a manageable amount, take a closer look at each of the properties. Buyers are out there looking at all the inventory. They will make close comparisons and will determine what to pay for a property, thus the market value of that property. So we must do the same.

In this example, there are two properties in the 2,000-total-square-feet range that sold in the $230,000 range, and there is another one that sold in the $165,000 range (just below the $170,000 price line). If two buyers were willing to pay $230,000 for a property while another buyer paid only $165,000, there must be a reason. To determine why the properties sold for different amounts, we have to go to the detailed MLS sheets. Once there, we focus first on hard-surface (flooring and countertops) upgrades and other features that create additional value in the customer's eyes. We also look for specific conditions that would lower the value for prospective buyers. Comments like "Needs TLC" or "Rented," or if the property was a distressed sale, are often major detractions to value.

After identifying the unique aspects of each property, we summarize those aspects for each of the properties on the graph in text boxes. We then often see the "pattern" and the Fair Market Value lines for each of those properties. Look at the updated graph to see the results of that analysis.

In the image on the following page, "2473 Leghorn" (the open circle) was the subject property I was pricing.

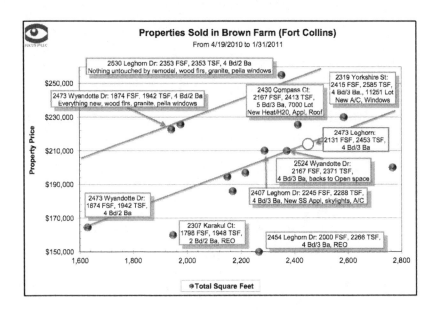

Properties Sold in Brown Farm (Fort Collins)
From 4/19/2010 to 1/31/2011

2530 Leghorn Dr: 2353 FSF, 2353 TSF, 4 Bd/2 Ba
Nothing untouched by remodel, wood firs, granite, pella windows

2319 Yorkshire St:
2415 FSF, 2585 TSF,
4 Bd/3 Ba., 11251 Lot
New A/C, Windows

2473 Wyandotte Dr: 1874 FSF, 1942 TSF, 4 Bd/2 Ba
Everything new, wood firs, granite, pella windows

2430 Compass Ct:
2167 FSF, 2413 TSF,
5 Bd/3 Ba, 7000 Lot
New Heat/H20, Appl, Roof

2473 Leghorn:
2131 FSF, 2453 TSF,
4 Bd/3 Ba

2524 Wyandotte Dr:
2167 FSF, 2371 TSF,
4 Bd/3 Ba, backs to Open space

2473 Wyandotte Dr:
1874 FSF, 1942 TSF,
4 Bd/2 Ba

2407 Leghorn Dr: 2245 FSF, 2288 TSF,
4 Bd/3 Ba, New SS Appl, skylights, A/C

2307 Karakul Ct:
1798 FSF, 1948 TSF,
2 Bd/2 Ba, REO

2454 Leghorn Dr: 2000 FSF, 2266 TSF,
4 Bd/3 Ba, REO

Property Price: $250,000 / $230,000 / $210,000 / $190,000 / $170,000 / $150,000

Total Square Feet: 1,600 / 1,800 / 2,000 / 2,200 / 2,400 / 2,600 / 2,800

●Total Square Feet

As you just saw, there are multiple trend lines. The top trend line shows the market value of the properties that have been remodeled or have significant upgrading. The second trend line shows the market value of the properties that haven't been upgraded but are in good shape and have some features. Properties that are well below the second trend line show properties where the condition is a problem. In this case, it shows distressed properties or foreclosure (REO) and short-sale properties.

This is a classic example of neighborhoods that are older. Older is relative but usually twenty years or more. Once homes start to age, buyers can tell a big difference in value between properties where sellers continue to update their homes and those where sellers have not. We also see multiple trend lines in neighborhoods where there is something different due to the location—for example, in neighborhoods where some homes are on the water, some homes are on a hill and have fantastic views, or some homes back up to greenbelts. These are all times where you can get multiple trend lines. Once you've determined the characteristic(s) of the trend line, you then need to determine whether the property you are pricing has that characteristic(s) or not. You can then see which trend line the subject property will fit on.

Let's quickly touch on what I said earlier about this not being a simple price-per-square-foot model. As you can see, although the trend line may use a similar calculation for its slope or angle, we are doing so much more than just relying on a plug-in formula. We are using the trend line and then a real and detailed comparison to find a truer value than simply going by square foot ever could.

In review, pricing your subject property against others is important in taking into effect factors one through five of pricing and pricing strategy. We do this by using the data for the last six months and plotting them on a scattergram. Remember to look for the Fair

Market Value (trend) line (the line going up and to the right) and then look at the scattergram graph to identify the outliers. Use this to figure out what about the outlier is causing it to be way off. Then when you price the subject property, determine if it is comparable to that, and if so, it too would need to be transposed from the trend line. Also, if there are several properties either above or below the line, there must be a reason. That reason can possibly be the same for all the properties and thus warrant another trend line.

7

Step 4: Position with "For Sales" and "Soon-to-Be For Sales"

Step 4: Position with "For Sales" and "Soon-to-Be For Sales"

Now that we have a baseline price, we are ready to move on to bringing in the seventh factor in pricing strategy: **Positioning**. We will see the sixth factor of pricing strategy, **Timing**, later when we get to Step 5. I know the factors are out of order, but have patience and you'll see the steps bring them back together perfectly.

Positioning is the process of putting your listing in the most competitively advantageous sweet spot. In simpler terms, putting it in a pricing position that makes it beat out the nearest competition in your buyer's mind. We want to make our homes sell before their comparable or at least not lose out. We are going to do this by seeing what the market looks like through the buyer's eyes. Here is the basic summary of the process or how to price a home while looking through a buyer's eyes.

Step 4.1

As a buyer will, look at the subject property and others that are comparably priced.

Step 4.2

Determine how many homes will sell in the respective price range in a defined period.

Step 4.3

Compare your home to others based on price, size, location, features and condition (the five factors of pricing).

Step 4.4

Look for competitive-advantage situations to put your listing in the "redzone."

Step 4.5

Adjust the price position of the property based on future competition.

Perform: Step 4.1 and Step 4.3

First we quickly examine homes in our area. We look at houses currently for sale or under contract in the neighborhood. Any that are for sale and all of the under contracts near our home's square-footage size in comparison make it to the short list.

Looking at the "For Sales," we want to avoid a situation where a house with more square footage is for sale for less money. Unless our listing is a gem and that home needs TLC, this puts our listing in a competitively disadvantageous position. We don't want that.

A quick note here: There may be situations where this happens, and it is not a bad thing, especially in neighborhoods with mixed construction dates, areas of high foreclosure rates or homes with unpermitted "finished" living areas. If this situation is coming up when comparing your initial price, then take a close look at those properties you are pricing against and decide how relevant they are to your pricing strategy. They may not be impactful, or they may completely change the landscape.

If your listing is larger in square feet and priced lower than the competition, you're in a good place to get some offers. If your listing is larger in square feet and higher in price, then this appears to follow the pattern but doesn't help you position the home. That's where the second area we look at comes into play.

As you know, when buyers are looking for a home, they aren't usually looking in only one neighborhood. They generally look at all different places in a certain price range. So we have more competition in the market, and it's time to make sure we aren't being supplanted by other properties in the buyer's mind. We are going to go back to the MLS and search for listings that are active and under contract in our price range.

First, let's use those under contract and compare and contrast them to the listing to see which we can beat and which we need to snuggle up to.

There is something to be said about under-contract homes. We need to examine those homes near our square footage and price to see how similar they are to our listing. Now, you could go super deep into this and do Steps 1–3 of Visual Pricing again for these properties and price them all to see how close they are to their baselines, but it's not necessary. This is the fine-tuning phase. You are simply focusing your efforts at this point. All you need to do is confirm your valuation ups and downs, and positioning. If you have adjusted the price up for the features and up even more because the positioning showed that you had room to stay in a competitive advantage in your neighborhood and be first off the market, those under contract and priced about the same should be a mirror of your listing. If not—if the homes priced the same or under contract are larger or in better conditions that your listing—then you need to be careful! If you are too closely related in price but not equal or better in perceived value you can shoot your sale in the foot.

We will do all of these comparisons by plotting on a scattergram again. Let's see what that would look like.

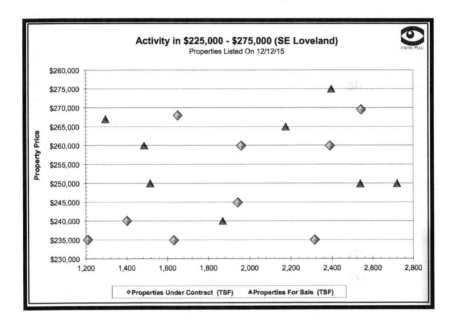

This scattergram shows the current competition in the $225,000-to-$275,000 price range in Southeast Loveland, Colorado. You can clearly see the current homes listed and their prospective square feet. Now let's imagine that the property we are pricing has 1,950 square feet, and our initial price range from our scattergram in the previous step had us looking at $250,000.

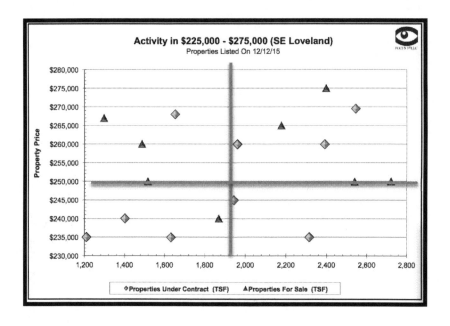

Activity in $225,000 - $275,000 (SE Loveland)
Properties Listed On 12/12/15

◇ Properties Under Contract (TSF)   ▲ Properties For Sale (TSF)

As you can see, we have some other homes listed at $250,000. One property has fewer square feet than our subject property, while two have more. If everything else were equal, location and condition, then we would be competitively advantaged to the lesser-square-foot property and competitively disadvantaged to the other two. Now let's say that after looking at those three MLS sheets, there are glaring differences, so they aren't going to affect us. Now let's look at the two under-contract properties close to our square footage. One is under contract at $245,000 and the other at $260,000. We would now look at the MLS sheets to figure out when they went under contract and how closely they resemble our property. They give a clear indication of the market, so if we match the $260,000 home closely, then we are going to adjust up to match it. Current information is better than past information.

Quickly, before we go further, let me cover **Step 4.2**. We have actually already covered this during our discussion of absorption rate in the first step of Visual Pricing. We will use this month's supply value and absorption rate as a guideline for adjustments as we decide how much range we want to play with in **Step 4.3**'s value movements. If the month's supply and absorption rate are telling us that the market is saturated, or crowded if you will, we don't want to be too aggressive. If the month's supply and absorption rate give us the green light, then we know we can really press for a little more value.

One important note: This month's supply and absorption rate that we found earlier was mainly for our area. Often it's wise to do another calculation using the search of price range in a given area. This allows for direct correlation between the positioning we are currently doing with active properties and the new absorption rate number.

Step 4.4

The redzone is the area of the graph that our property has a competitive advantage over. Generally we try to guide our properties so that our nearest competition falls into this area. Continuing with the previous example graph but changing our square footage slightly, let's take a look at the redzone. Note that we are changing our square footage to around 1,600 square feet, and our initial pricing trend-line adjustments led us to $252,000.

In that area, our larger square footage and price of $252,000 make a winning combination over the redzone. All else being equal among the competition, we would be the first to get an offer in most cases and not be stuck on the market. Let's look at the graph to visualize this:

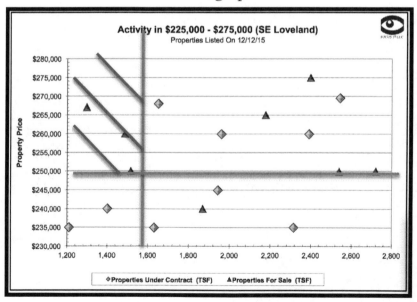

You can see here that we could adjust our price up to nearly $260,000 and still have a competitive advantage to both properties in the redzone. The other home for sale at $250,000 is fewer square feet, so we may tie them for perceived value as we raise the price; therefore, we still need to be careful about getting too wild. If we kept the price at $250,000, we would have current market dominance. I say "current market" because new entrants are coming, and they are looking to change the game. So far, we have been looking at all *current information*. There is only one thing better than looking at current information: being able to tell the future. That's where **Step 4.5** comes along.

Step 4.2 and 4.5

To better explain looking at future competition, let's listen to a story and teaching from Tim DeLeon, creator of Visual Pricing and the Visual Pricing System as well as an accomplished real estate agent himself.

Tim DeLeon

*I live in Fort Collins, which is about sixty miles north of Denver in Colorado. In March of 2015, my niece (who lives south of Denver) called me, asking for my help. Unbeknownst to me, she had been looking around her mom's (my sister's) neighborhood for homes so that she could move closer to her. She had just walked into an open house and found the house of her dreams. The owner told her she would take an offer from her if she could get her home sold **over the upcoming weekend!** So she frantically dialed my number, asking me if I could sell her home in **two days**. Wow. My immediate response was, "I don't know. Let me look at it. I'll get back to you on that."*

My niece's house was in Highlands Ranch, which is an area south of Denver. In most cases, this is business that I would refer to one of many of the great real estate agents that are there, as it is outside my usual sphere, about sixty minutes' drive. Listing a home that distance away (not to mention my lack of knowledge of the area) would not be something that I would recommend anyone doing. However, since I had only the upcoming weekend to get her home under contract, I took a look at the situation using the Visual Pricing System. Understanding "where the puck is going" was critical to my success.

The concept of "going where the puck is going" is based on the response from "The Great One"—Wayne Gretzky—when he was asked by a reporter why he was so good. His response was that while the effectiveness of a hockey player was determined by how quickly he could get to the puck to make a play, he (Wayne Gretzky) was so great because he didn't go where the puck was, but he went to where the puck was going. Now while that might be a great sound bite—and obviously, it's a change of mindset if you're a hockey player trying to get to the puck—the big challenge is, "How do you know where the puck is going to be?"

Of course, knowing where the puck is going to be requires a tremendous amount of study of formations, plays that the opposition uses, the strengths and weaknesses of each of the individual opposition players, the players on your team and a ton of experience. So while "going where the puck is going" depends on a fundamental mindset change, it required a tremendous amount of additional professionalism to really be able to act on that mindset. This is a great analogy with real estate.

If Wayne Gretzky were a real estate agent, he would say, "I don't price properties on where the market is. I price properties on where the market is going to be." Of course, just like the hockey analogy, the challenge is first the mindset. However, once you have the mindset change, then you have to get the skill set in motion as well. That is, once you've decided to price properties based on where the market is going, you then have to figure out where the market is going.

There are several models that agents have used to do this. My personal favorite has become the Real Estate Pond. The Real Estate Pond was developed by James Reese of Carolina One. This is a great model for helping people who have difficulty with graphs and need something more practical for perspective. It makes the analogy between real estate (with homes coming on and off the market) and water flowing into and out of a pond. If the flow of water going into the pond is the same as the flow of water going out of the pond, you have a balanced market. If the flow of water going into the pond exceeds the flow leaving, your pond starts to fill up. This is the case when you have more homes (inventory) coming on the market than the homes that are selling in a *period of time, and you have an excess supply of properties on the market. In this case, you move into a buyer's market.*

Of course, if the flow of water leaving the pond exceeds the flow entering, your pond starts to empty. This is the case when you have more homes selling than the homes that are being listed in a period of time. You then have less inventory of properties than needed to supply the upcoming demand. In this case, you move into a seller's market.

First I created a pond based on the data I pulled from the MLS and used that to identify the market. This pond is based on the activity for the last three months (for this example).

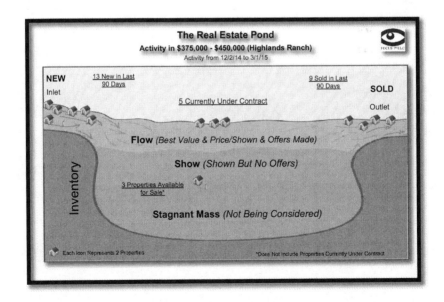

We don't know for sure what will happen in the next three months, but by using the Pricing Pond, we can assume that the next three months will be comparable to this pattern. Using that assumption, I created a Projected Pond.

The Projected Pond looks comparable and works the same as the Real Estate Pond except that it includes the adjustments we've been talking about. It makes the adjustments or corrections for the market trends and the seasonality. This tool by itself makes a tremendous impact and allows you to know where the "puck" is going. Once you know where the puck is going and you know what the supply and demand looks like, you will be able to create an effective pricing strategy to allow your customers to price their property to sell for the most value.

In the pricing process I focused on the area, while in the positioning search, I expanded the area and focused on the price range. This is because, from a buyer's perspective, I knew they would be focusing on a price range that they were qualified to purchase, and while they would be looking in my niece's neighborhood, they would also be looking outside the neighborhood, in surrounding areas as well. So I also wanted to include those areas yet still maintain the price range.

Take a look at the chart I discovered when looking at all the homes and the "supply and demand" using the Projected Pond for the expanded area surrounding my niece's home in the $375,000-to-$425,000 price range.

As you will see, there were currently five homes under contract and an additional three properties for sale (shown below the homes under contract). Then, looking to the right, you will see that the projected sales for the next three months showed eighteen properties. Of course, five of those eighteen were already under contract, so that would leave an additional thirteen properties to sell within the next three months.

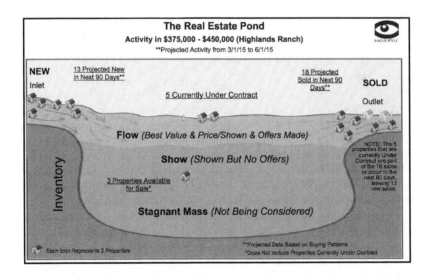

With the demand of thirteen properties to sell in the next three months and the supply of only three properties for

sale, there was a huge supply and demand in her favor. Of course, we will also notice that an additional thirteen properties would be coming on the market in the next three months as well. The challenge (which was an easy one in her case) was to get on the market before the other thirteen competitors. Based on this information alone, I was convinced that we could get her house sold over the weekend. Actually, with this information, I felt that we could get multiple offers.

That feeling, and the pricing strategy we built based on the Visual Pricing Process, dictated that we do a listing launch. A listing launch, or putting the house on the market and announcing we will look at all offers in two days, is a risky, hot-or-cold option because it can turn off potential buyers. I was extremely nervous about it, but I trusted the data and recommended that option. The Projected Pond and the Visual Pricing Process told me I should.

*After a few hand-wringing days, we had not received one offer—**WE HAD RECEIVED SEVEN!** All seven were above list price, and the contract we settled on had even guaranteed appraisal. Talk about being grateful that I listened to the pattern.*

—Tim DeLeon

If you don't happen to have the great tool of the Visual Pricing System and don't want to draw a pond by hand, we can look at future competition quickly in a simpler manner that will allow us to gauge how to temper our value adjustments.

To anticipate the future competition, we are going to look at the number of listings that have been coming on the market over the last few months. Simply count on your MLS search, of the similar price range, the number for each month and total them up.

Now we are going to look at how many closed every month for the last few months as well. We do this by counting the number that closed.

Now count those that are currently for sale.

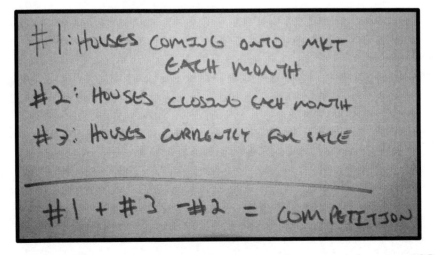

These three numbers show the flow in and out of the market for homes. In most cases, you'll find that the number of new entrants is higher than the number of sales. What this means is that there is a chance you might not sell, but we knew that. What these numbers show as well is the activity in the market. If the number is high, then it's a highly commoditized market, and pricing uniquely will be punished. Pricing with too much adjustment will put you in a difficult position.

If the activity is less, then it's a specialized market. This means that adjustments are more impactful and the homes are more unique. But this also shows you that the number of buyers out there is going to be less. This will be an important point for your strategy.

8

Step 5: Connecting & combining steps 1- 4

Step 5: Connecting and Combining Steps 1 – 4

It's strategy-building time!

So far, we have made patterns that answer key customer questions. These patterns, however, are only insights into different aspects of a single larger problem, or pieces to one puzzle, if you will. Now it's time to assemble the pieces and put this jigsaw together to form the big picture.

We are going to start at our baseline-adjusted price. This is the value we have come up with by using recent past home sales and comparing their positives and negatives. We found this base price using our trend line and adjusting up and down. The question then becomes, "Is this the right price for the current market, or do I need to move it down? Do I have room to reach for more?" To assess this, we will look at our positioning results.

Are we in a competitive-advantage positioning compared to the other homes on the market? Are we in a competitive disadvantage? Let's say, for example, we are in a good "sweet spot" as far as current competition goes. Now let's look at how many competitors are going to be coming in on average. Are there a lot, or are we a little more rare? If this type of home is commonly coming up for sale, we probably don't want to adjust much higher, because a lot of others are coming. We need to get off the market while we are still alpha dog. Let's go back and use the example of being a little more rare. Now we know that there isn't much competition coming in and disrupting the market, but does that mean we can go up, or do we need to go down because this house may not sell easily? Well, is this the right time for this property to be selling? Adjust up. Or are we in a no-buy window? Probably list at a lower price or a later time. To judge this, we are going to look at the timing patterns all the way back in Step 1 and bring in that long-lost pricing-strategy factor: **Timing.**

The odds-of-selling graph will tell us if this type of home sells or if the chances don't look good. The time-to-sell graph will show us if price in this neighborhood extends the time it takes to sell. This can be super important! Why? We need the third pattern for that answer. The neighborhood buying pattern shows the best time—and sometimes the only time—for this house to sell. Well we need to know that if we reach for a few extra dollars, it extends the time to sell by thirty days and puts us in a no-buy window. These "windows" I'm referring to are the buying pattern best-selling times we looked at earlier, just to be clear. If the price has no effect on time to sell but we are currently in a time that fewer homes in our area sell, then we can't be going up too much, if at all. Breaking the pattern and being one of the rare properties to sell has a cost. You must pay the troll to pass the bridge, and the toll costs some of your list price.

So now that we have used the adjusted base price, found a sweet spot in today's market and positioned the property based on the competition and timing aspect of the market, we can say that we have a complete price. We have strategically placed the home in the best place for its sale. So is that the pricing strategy? It's half of it. We are building this strategy for two reasons. The first, which is to price the home accurately, is what we just accomplished. The second is to prepare the sellers for what is coming in the transaction.

The constructing of a strategy gives us the ability to be ready to react to changes or challenges that may arise. This mobility allows for the home to sell even if there are unforeseen troubles. More importantly, this strategic approach prepares your sellers for the unknown.

If the market suddenly cools or buyers go on strike, you won't have to worry about asking for a price drop, because that was built into your strategy. If you aren't under contract in two weeks and the time-to-sell average for your homes area is eighty days, then it's probably time to adjust fast! Conversely, if the average is 150 days and you're not under contract within the first week, your seller won't be as nervous because you will have prepared them for this possibility. They understand that their area is supposed to take longer and have planned accordingly.

If your sellers are flexible and the home clearly has a better market window in its neighborhood pattern coming in two months, asking them to wait won't be such a strange feeling.

The added bonus is that your sellers won't fight you about the price or why you can't list it for $20,000 more and just see what happens. You already know what happens. I don't know about you, but the eradication of the following conversation is a personal goal of mine.

Customer: *I understand everything you're saying.*

You: *Awesome! Let's sign the paperwork, and we'll get this baby sold.*

Customer: *Perfect, except let's list for $30,000 more.*

You (Confused): *Do we need to go over the pricing again?*

Customer: *No, I hear you, but let's just try it, huh? Worst that can happen is, we adjust it down later.*

You (Internally): *Worst that can happen is, we don't sell. Just wait until we do need to price cut, because the house isn't going to sell for that, and you'll start asking what I'm doing to sell the house.*

You: *Yeah, we can't do that.*

Customer: *Why not?*

You: *Let's go over the pricing again.*

This is something that needs to stop. I am not sure about you, but for me, that conversation was beyond irritating, it felt disrespectful. I know it's not meant that way, but it was a vote of no confidence for my work. Well if you use a pricing strategy, they can understand your recommendation. You have led them down the path to pricing enlightenment.

The question you may ask, and should be asking, here is, "How do I present all of this to them?" That really is where the magic happens, and to answer that, you'll have to keep reading. It's time for Step 6 to be revealed.

Step 6: Make It Visual

9

Step 6: Make it Visual

Step 6: Make It Visual

While Step 6 may be the end of our journey together in this book, it is probably the most important. The final factor of pricing strategy that we must address is **Understanding**. While this factor is independent of pricing, it is a key to pricing strategy.

This last step allows all of your work to actually mean something.

Have you ever priced a home perfectly yet, for some reason, your sellers seem to push back against your recommendations? Maybe they want to sell for more. Maybe they don't think their house is worth that much and are nervous about listing for such a grand number and not selling. Both of these situations can be difficult to negotiate because they are emotionally charged with fear—fear of losing out on money they could have had or fear of not selling.

These fears are coming from confusion. You must eliminate that confusion and replace it with knowledge and confidence.

The easiest way to lead them down the pricing-strategy path is to show them the way. Be their tour guide. This isn't that hard either. Simply show them what you did. *Show them!*

Take the patterns you've made and make them visual in some way. We understand things we see much easier. Let me ask you, how did you understand the message of this book? Was it really the thousands of words in its pages or the patterns and graphs you saw? Patterns are much easier to understand visually than by explaining with words.

Think about trying to explain an M.C. Escher pattern picture.

There are black birds flying. They turn into frogs with edges, then into butterflies, then into some kind of lizard, and then into white hearts. You came up with an image in your mind just now, but is it the one I wanted you to see? Probably not. But if I showed you a picture, you would be on the same page.

To prove this point...

Here is another Scattergram.

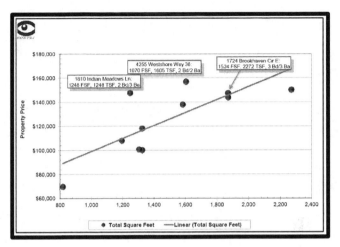

Scattergram

I'll bet you can easily look at that graph and tell me where a home should be priced! Visuals are king!

Did you know that in most cases of a competitive-listing situation, the "sales pitch" from real estate agents (their marketing plan, company info, etc.) is forgotten. What's not forgotten? Their pricing pictures! We know this because real estate professionals we have taught the Visual Pricing Process tell us the same story over and over again.

"The graphs are memorable, and people get excited by them!"

"They signed on with me because they loved my pricing!"

117

So you must make your presentation visual. Make graphics and graphs that show the patterns of the steps. Put them together in the same order as the steps and walk your clients through them. Let them walk the Visual Pricing Process with you, and together your strategy will help the home sell. If the home sells and you get that client where they need to be, your business will grow. Your job is to sell homes by accurately pricing them for sale.

"Pricing is one place you can really shine."
— Larry Kendall, Founder of Ninja Selling Inc.

Thank you so much for taking the time to read this book. I truly hope that it helps you price homes and land more listings. If you do find the words in its pages helpful, I ask that you help others find this book by reviewing it on Amazon.com.

Sincerely,
Jonathan DeLeon

The graphs shown in this book were created using the Visual Pricing System from Focus 1ˢᵗ LLC.

To learn more, visit www.focus1st.com.

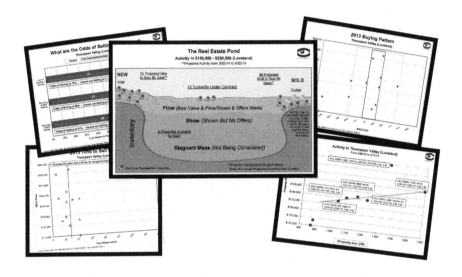

Use the code " VISUALPRICINGBOOK " at checkout for a special new subscriber discount!

About the Authors

Tim DeLeon was born July 31, 1954, in Pueblo, Colorado. Tim entered real estate following a twenty-five-year career at Hewlett-Packard, developing software products. He found that he loved real estate but that there was no software out there to really help a person accurately price a home and then show a customer why. Embracing the motto of "Showing is better than telling!" Tim created Scattergram Pricing. Soon after, he created the Neighborhood Buying Patterns and the rest of the tools that now make up the Visual Pricing System.

Using the tools to create success in his own real estate career, Tim is now helping thousands of real estate agents across the nation by providing quality tools and education that help price homes accurately, and quickly.

Jonathan DeLeon was born January 29, 1989, in Fort Collins, Colorado. After graduation from Colorado State University, he worked for Focus 1st LLC for six months before selling real estate at The Group, Inc. Real Estate in Fort Collins. Following a successful year, he moved into self-help writing and rejoined Focus 1st LLC. He now works for Focus 1st LLC as a business development manager, is a Level 1 CrossFit Trainer and has written several works on the topics of real estate, weight loss and science fiction. He has brought this storytelling and teaching side of his personality to Focus 1st LLC to help real estate agents.

The Visual Pricing Process

1. **Know the Subject Property**
   a. Use a map search to analyze outside and layout of property.
   b. Use past MLS sheet and public records to learn inside facts.
   c. Use a personal visit to look at condition details and any major changes.

2. **Know the Neighborhood**
   a. Use past year's information to establish an odds of selling.
   b. Use past sales to build a neighborhood buying pattern.
   c. Use past sales to find an average time to sale.

3. **Compare to Recent "Solds"**
   a. Use last six months' "Solds" to establish a baseline.
   b. Use baseline to set initial price.
   c. Compare to close-proximity properties to make initial adjustments.

4. **Position with "For Sales" and "Soon-to-Be For Sales"**
   a. Position the property to be in a competitively advantageous market position.

5. **Connect It All Together**
   a. Use all the patterns to fine-tune your pricing and create a strategy for possible future events. (Ex: If the average time to sale is 60 days and nothing is selling after 70 days, you better be taking active price action if you're not under contract in 15 days. 15 Days on Market + 45 Average Contract Length = 60 Days)

6. **Make It Visual**
   a. Turn your patterns and information into visuals that you can walk your customers through.

Pre Listing Interview

"If it is alright with you, I would like to ask you a few questions and then set up a time for us to get together. These questions are to help me prepare for our meeting and should take about 10 minutes. Is this an okay time with you?"

1. Name _____

2. Property Address _____
    Mailing Address _____

3. Owners/Decision Makers _____
    Phone (H) _____ (B) _____ (C) _____
    Fax _____ Email _____

4. Why are you selling? _____

5. When do you need to move? _____

6. Could you describe your house for me? _____
    Beds _____ Baths _____ Sq. Ft _____
    Style _____ Lot Size _____ Bsmt? _____

7. How long have you owned your home? _____

8. What sold you on your home when you bought it? What features
    did you like? _____
    _____
    _____

9. Have you done any updating to the home since you bought it?
    _____
    _____
    _____

10. If you were to stay in your home another 5 years, is there anything you
    would do to it? _____
    _____
    _____
    _____

Printed with permission from Ninja Selling, LLC. www.ninjaselling.com

Trend Line Calculating by Hand

The trend line will establish a set starting point from which to apply our adjustments. By having this starting point, we are able to be much more accurate and consistent in our pricing.

To build this trend line by hand, we are going back to early algebra class. We will find a line that can be used to approximate a square-foot-to-price relationship. This is the formula for a line:

$$Y = mx + b$$

We are going to take the price per square foot of all the homes sold in the last six months and average them. This will be our slope for the line or "m."

$$Y = \left(\text{Average Price Per FT}^2 \right) x + b$$

Next we are going to use that "m" to find the line by entering the information from one of our sold houses.

$$\text{SALE PRICE} = (\text{AVERAGE PRICE PER FT}^2)(\text{SQUARE FEET}) + b$$

$$b = \text{SALE PRICE} - (\text{AVERAGE PRICE PER FT}^2)(\text{SQUARE FEET})$$

Now we have a baseline that we can use to establish a point to adjust from for our house pricing. We take the property we want to price and put its information for square foot into the formula and find a baseline price.

$$\text{BASELINE PRICE}$$

$$(\text{AVERAGE PRICE PER FT}^2)(\text{SUBJECT PROPERTY FT}^2) + b$$

Then we adjust up and down by comparing it to the homes that have sold close to this price, above and below. We are looking more for similarities than differences at this point so that we can establish what is most comparable about these properties. Once we have found a home that is much akin to the property we are pricing, we will use it to determine the initial jump above or drop below the baseline.

We will take that property and use its square footage to establish a baseline price.

We then take the difference between the baseline price and the actual price the home sold for.

ACTUAL SALE PRICE − BASELINE PRICE

INITIAL PRICE ADJUSTMENT

This then becomes our base price difference or initial price adjustment. Now we have a baseline price and an initial price adjustment for our subject property. Combining these two numbers leads to our first pricing-strategy maneuver.

Once we have maneuvered our home to a higher or lower price to more correctly establish its correlation to a like comparable home, we will look at what's different between the two. This is where we can adjust more and fine-tune the pricing, and where some subjectivity on your part comes in. However, make adjustments according to your expertise.

This is done by looking at the two MLS sheets side by side. *Here is where you will use your sheet of notes about the property as well as the rest of the information from Step 1: Know the Subject Property.

Keep in mind that this only covers key factors two through five in our pricing-strategy model, so we are going to adjust price more as we continue to build this process, but it is still important to accomplish this part accurately.

If done correctly, we will have accounted for location **(already used in the previous step)**, price, size, special features and amenities.

Again, here is a visual to show you in a simpler form what this step is doing. This graph is a scattergram that shows the trend line as well as several comparable properties. You can easily see how we examine the graph to help establish a starting point for our analysis of the subject property.

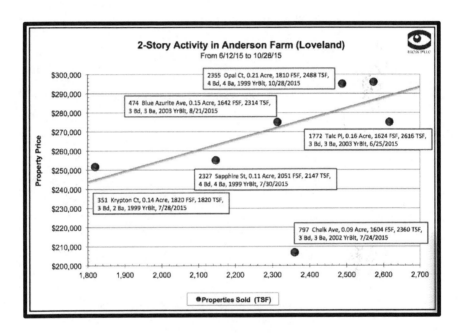

Want more knowledge about pricing?
Check out our YouTube Channel at:
www.youtube.com/focus1stllc

Made in the USA
San Bernardino, CA
16 January 2020